MY ALEXANDRIA

MY ALEXANDRIA

Mark Doty

CAPE POETRY

First published 1995

1 3 5 7 9 10 8 6 4 2

© Mark Doty 1995

Mark Doty has asserted his right
under the Copyright, Designs and Patents Act, 1988
to be identified as the author of this work

First published in the United Kingdom in 1995 by
Jonathan Cape
Random House, 20 Vauxhall Bridge Road, London SW1V 2SA

Random House Australia (Pty) Limited
20 Alfred Street, Milsons Point, Sydney,
New South Wales 2061, Australia

Random House New Zealand Limited
18 Poland Road, Glenfield,
Auckland 10, New Zealand

Random House South Africa (Pty) Limited
PO Box 337, Bergvlei, South Africa

Random House UK Limited Reg. No. 954009

A CIP catalogue record for this book
is available from the British Library

ISBN 0–224–04128–2

Phottypeset by Intype, London
Printed in Great Britain by
Mackays of Chatham PLC

Anyone else may leave you, I will never leave you, fugitive.
— Jean Valentine

CONTENTS

ACKNOWLEDGEMENTS

Grateful acknowledgements to the editors of the following magazines, in which these poems first appeared, sometimes in earlier versions:

The American Voice, Boulevard, Folio, Green Mountains Review, Indiana Review, James White Review, Mid-American Review, The Missouri Review, One Meadway, Outweek, Passages North, Ploughshares, Poetry, Southwest Review

'Bill's Story' appeared in *Poets for Life: Seventy-six Poets Respond to AIDS*, 1989, and in *The Pushcart Prize XIV: Best of the Small Presses*. 'Heaven' and 'Night Ferry' appeared in *New American Poets of the 90s*. 'Difference' appeared in *The Best American Poetry 1994*.

My gratitude, as well, to Mark Cox, Kathryn Davis, Lynda Hull, Philip Levine and the staff at the University of Illinois Press for their irreplaceable help with this book.

DEMOLITION

The intact façade's now almost black
in the rain; all day they've torn at the back
of the building, 'the oldest concrete structure
in New England,' the newspaper said. By afternoon,
when the backhoe claw appears above
three storeys of columns and cornices,

the crowd beneath their massed umbrellas cheer.
Suddenly the stairs seem to climb down themselves,
atomized plaster billowing: dust of 1907's
rooming house, this year's bake shop and florist's,
the ghosts of their signs faint above the windows
lined, last week, with loaves and blooms.

We love disasters that have nothing to do
with us: the metal scoop seems shy, tentative,
a Japanese monster tilting its yellow head
and considering what to topple next. It's a weekday,
and those of us with the leisure to watch
are out of work, unemployable or academics,

joined by a thirst for watching something fall.
All summer, at loose ends, I've read biographies,
Wilde and Robert Lowell, and fallen asleep
over a fallen hero lurching down a Paris boulevard,
talking his way to dinner or a drink,
unable to forget the vain and stupid boy

he allowed to ruin him. And I dreamed
I was Lowell, in a manic flight of failing
and ruthless energy, and understood
how wrong I was with a passionate exactitude
which had to be like his. A month ago,

I

at Saint-Gauden's house, we ran from a startling
    downpour

into coincidence: under a loggia built
for performances on the lawn
hulked Shaw's monument, splendid
in its plaster maquette, the ramrod-straight colonel
high above his black troops. We crouched on wet gravel
and waited out the squall; the hieratic woman

– a wingless angel? – floating horizontally
above the soldiers, her robe billowing like plaster dust,
seemed so far above us, another century's
allegorical decor, an afterthought
who'd never descend to the purely physical
soldiers, the nearly breathing bronze ranks crushed

into a terrible compression of perspective,
as if the world hurried them into the ditch.
'The unreadable,' Wilde said, 'is what occurs.'
And when the brutish metal rears
above the wall of unglazed windows –
where, in a week, the kids will skateboard

in their lovely loops and spray
their indecipherable ideograms
across the parking lot – the single standing wall
seems Roman, momentarily, an aqueduct,
all that's left of something difficult
to understand now, something Oscar

and Bosie might have posed before, for a photograph.
Aqueducts and angels, here on Main,
seem merely souvenirs; the gaps
where the windows opened once

into transients' rooms are pure sky.
It's strange how much more beautiful

the sky is to us when it's framed
by these columned openings someone meant us
to take for stone. The enormous, articulate shovel
nudges the highest row of mouldings
and the whole thing wavers as though we'd dreamed it,
our black classic, and it topples all at once.

HEAVEN

Tonight there's a mirror on the sidewalk,
  leaning on the steps of the cathedral.
    I want to think it's a work of art,
      or at least an intentional gesture:

anyone passing can see, reversed here,
  the rooftop Virgin's golden face
    ringed by lightbulbs, looking up toward *us*.
      A few blocks down the searchlights revolve

atop some office tower's steely sheen.
  Where would they lead us, these beacons
    that sweep the dark and cut the steam
      billowing from the stacks, so the sudden sections

of cloud tumble in stunning and troubled currents?
  I have a friend who sometimes sells
    everything, scrapes together enough money
      to get to the city, and lives on the streets here,

in the parks. She says she likes waking
  knowing she can be anyone she wants, keep any name
    as long as it wears well. She stayed with one man
      a few days; calling themselves whatever they liked

or nothing, they slept in the park
  beneath a silver cloth, a 'space blanket'
    that mirrored the city lights, and the heat
      of his dog coiled between them would warm them.

I knew, she says, *I was in heaven.*
  Isn't that where those beams washing
    and disguising the stars have always called us:

4

the anonymous paradise, where there isn't any
  telling

how many of these futures
  will be ours? It was enough to be warmed
    by steam blurring the café windows, to study
      how grocers stacked the wet jewels

of produce and seem fed – though the wine-flush
  would brighten everything, and dull the morning
    of working a thankless block. She held out her hand
      enough times to catch a torrent,

though little was offered but the sharpening chill
  of the street lacquered by rain, perfected
    and unyielding. *It's a little easier*
      for a woman to panhandle; that's why

my friend needed the dog. Sometime,
  when the weather turned, she'd go back home,
    at least till spring. Longer,
      maybe. But not before arriving at afternoons

when she wanted nothing, whole nights
  without desire, since everything passing
    was hers. Though she could not participate
      in the mortal pretence of keeping anything;

that lie belonged to the privileged,
  who hurried along the sidewalks
    just outside the stone boundaries of the park.
      And though they tried to warm themselves with it,

they still required those luxurious,
  frost-tipped pelts, the skins ripped and tailored

out of their contexts. She knew she could lie there, with her stranger, with the living animal between them.

DAYS OF 1981

Cambridge Street, summer,
and a boy in a blue bandanna brought the bartender
flowers: delphiniums, splendid, blackened

in the dim room, though it was still afternoon, 'tea
dance', in the heat of early July. Men in too-tight jeans
– none of them dancing – watched

the black women singing. Secret advocates of our hearts,
they urged us on as they broke apart
in painterly chaos on the video screen,

gowns and wigs, perfectly timed gestures
becoming bits of iridescent weather
in the club's smoked atmosphere. The Supremes

– by then historical, lushly ascetic – then the endless
stream of women we loved, emblematic, reckless
in their attachments, or so the songs would have us think.

The man I met, slight and dark as Proust, a sultry flirt,
introduced himself because he liked my yellow shirt.
I don't remember who bought who drinks,

or why I liked him; I think it was simply
that I *could*. The heady rush of quickly
leaving together, late sun glaring over the Charles,

those last white sails blinding: it was so easy,
and strangely exhilarating, and free
as the woman singing: a tidal, glimmering whirl

into which you could ease down, without thinking,
and simply be swept away. I was ready and waiting
to be swept. After the subway ride,

he knelt in front of me on the bleachers
in an empty suburban park, and I reached
for anything to hold onto, my head thrown back

to blueblack sky rinsed at the rim
with blazing city lights, then down to him:
relentless, dazzling, anyone. The smokestacks

and office towers loomed, a half-lit backdrop
beyond the baseball diamond. I didn't want him to ever
    stop,
and he left me breathless and unsatisfied.

He was a sculptor, and for weeks afterward I told myself
I loved him, because I'd met a man and wasn't sure
I could meet another – I'd never tried –

and because the next morning, starting
off to work, the last I saw of him, he gave me a heart,
ceramic, the marvel of a museum school show

his class had mounted. No one could guess
how he'd fired hollow clay entirely seamless
and kept it from exploding. I thought it beautiful, though

I was wrong about so much: him,
my prospects, the charm of the gift.
Out of context, it was a cool,

lumpish thing, earth-toned, lop-sided,
incapable of standing on its own. I propped
it up with books, then left it somewhere, eventually,

though I don't mind thinking of it now,
when I don't have the first idea where it's gone.
I called him more than twice.

If I knew where he was, even his last name,
(something French?) I might call again
to apologise for my naive

persistence, my lack of etiquette,
my ignorance of the austere code of tricks.
I didn't know then how to make love like that.

I thought of course we'd go on learning
the fit of chest to chest, curve to curve.
I didn't understand the ethos, the drama

of the search,
the studied approach to touch
as brief and recklessly enjambed

as the magic songs: *Give me just a little more time,*
I'm so excited, I will survive.
Nothing was promised, nothing sustained

or lethal offered. I wish I'd kept the heart.
Even the emblems of our own embarrassment
become acceptable to us, after a while,

evidence of someone we'd once have wished to erase:
a pottery heart,
an unrecaptured thing that might represent

the chancy exhilaration of a day, years ago
– *1981* – bleached sails on the Charles blowing,
the blueblack women in their rapture on the screen,

their perfected longing and release.
The astonishing flowers, seething
a blue I could barely see.

HUMAN FIGURES

On the Number Fifteen bus on Portrero Hill,
San Francisco, a morning of clouds shifting
like ripples on silk, a black man
a few seats in front of me covers his lap

with Chinese newspapers and smooths
the rumpled sheets across his thighs
over and over. I think he's hiding
something beneath them, himself perhaps,

until looking directly out the windows
with their clouds he begins to tear
the sheets of newspaper in half
and rolls the delicate black moss

of calligraphy into a cone, twists it
into something intricate between his broad hands,
something he doesn't want anyone to see.
Then he places whatever he's made

on the seat beside him and covers it,
covertly, with another sheet of news,
and tears and rolls, furiously, as though
he can't make one thing and leave it alone.

I think he's seen me watching,
and I try not to look as he keeps
rolling faster, till we reach a stop
and a quick gust of wind from the door

lifts the paper veil just enough to reveal
what he's made. Once, in Boston,
a vagrant lay on one of the long stone benches
by the Public Library, bleeding.

I don't know what had happened;
a little crescent of people clustered,
waiting for the ambulance
to work its way through traffic.

I didn't want to be like them,
didn't want to look, and a sheet of newspaper,
a page of the *Globe* ripping down Boylston,
skittered across the red slick of him and tumbled

toward me, the stain already drying
on four columns of news. Soon
it wouldn't even be recognisable,
the blood in its morning edition

blowing across my shoes. Suppose the ambulance
hadn't come and he'd kept on bleeding,
a stain larger than his own body
darkening the cement and all the paper

blown along those windy steps?
Imagine he'd kept on publishing himself
until his outline were larger than anything
the police could chalk, uncontained,

the shapeless bulletin of the news you can't buy,
though you can't help but read it.
And the man in San Francisco twists his papers
into dolls, tiny human forms –

like ginseng roots floating
in Chinatown windows, long limbs streaming out
behind them – figures moulded
into something intimate, something to hide.

ALMOST BLUE

Chet Baker, 1929–1988

If Hart Crane played trumpet
he'd sound like you, your horn's dark city

miraculous and broken over and over,
scale-shimmered, every harbour-flung hour

and salt-span of cabled longing,
every waterfront, the night-lovers' rendezvous.

This is the entrance
to the city of you, sleep's hellgate,

and two weeks before the casual relinquishment
of your hold – light needling

on the canal's gleaming haze
and the buds blaring like horns –

two weeks before the end, Chet,
and you're playing like anything,

singing *stay little valentine
stay*

and taking so long there are worlds sinking
between the notes, this exhalation

no longer a voice but a rush of air,
brutal, from the tunnels under the river,

the barges' late whistles you only hear
when the traffic's stilled

by snow, a city hushed and
distilled into one rush of breath,

yours, into the microphone
and the ear of that girl

in the leopard-print scarf,
one long kiss begun on the highway

and carried on dangerously,
the Thunderbird veering

on the coast road: glamour
of a perfectly splayed fender,

dazzling lipstick, a little pearl of junk,
some stretch of road breathless

and travelled into . . . Whoever she is
she's the other coast of you,

and just beyond the bridge the city's
long amalgam of ardour and indifference

is lit like a votive
then blown out. Too many rooms unrented

in this residential hotel,
and you don't want to know

why they're making that noise in the hall;
you're going to wake up in any one of the

how many ten thousand
locations of trouble and longing

going out of business forever everything must go
wake up and start wanting.

It's so much better when you don't want:
nothing falls then, nothing lost

but sleep and who wanted that
in the pearl this suspended world is,

in the warm suspension and glaze
of this song everything stays up

almost forever in the long
glide sung into the vein,

one note held almost impossibly
almost blue and the lyric takes so long

to open, a little blood
blooming: *there's no love song   finer*

*but how strange the change
from major to minor*

*everytime
we say goodbye*

and you leaning into that warm
haze from the window, Amsterdam,

late afternoon glimmer
a blur of buds

breathing in the lindens
and you let go and why not

ESTA NOCHE

In a dress with a black tulip's sheen
   la fabulosa Lola enters, late, mounts the stairs
to the plywood platform, and begs whoever runs
   the wobbling spot to turn the lights down

to something flattering. When they halo her
   with a petal-toned gel, she sets to haranguing,
shifting in and out of two languages like gowns
   or genders to *please* have a little respect

for the girls, flashing the one entrancing
   and unavoidable gap in the centre of her upper teeth.
And when the cellophane drop goes black,
   a new spot coronas her in a wig

fit for the end of a century,
   and she tosses back her hair – risky gesture –
and raises her arms like a widow in a blood tragedy,
   all will and black lace, and lipsyncs 'You and Me

against the World'. She's a man
   you wouldn't look twice at in street clothes,
two hundred pounds of hard living, the gap in her smile
   sadly narrative – but she's a monument,

in the mysterious permission of the dress.
   This is Esta Noche, a Latin drag bar in the Mission,
its black door a gap in the face
   of a battered wall. All over the neighbourhood

storefront windows show all night
   shrined hats and gloves, wedding dresses,
First Communion's frothing lace:
   gowns of perfection and commencement,

fixed promises glowing. In the dress
 the colour of the spaces between streetlamps
Lola stands unassailable, the dress
 in which she is in the largest sense

fabulous: a lesson, a criticism and colossus
 of gender, all fire and irony. Her spine's
perfectly erect, only her fluid hands moving
 and her head turned slightly to one side.

She hosts the pageant, Wednesdays and Saturdays
 and men come in from the streets, the trains,
and the repair shops, lean together to rank
 the artifice of the awkward or lovely

Lola welcomes onto the stage: Victoria, Elena,
 Francie, lamé pumps and stockings and always
the rippling night pulled down over broad shoulders
 and flounced around the hips, liquid,

the black silk of esta noche
 proving that perfection and beauty are so alien
they almost never touch. Tonight, she says,
 put it on. The costume is licence

and calling. She says you could wear the whole damn
 black sky and all its spangles. It's the only night
we have to stand on. Put it on,
 it's the only thing we have to wear.

BROADWAY

Under Grand Central's tattered vault
  – maybe half a dozen electric stars still lit –
    one saxophone blew, and a sheer black scrim

billowed over some minor constellation
  under repair. Then, on Broadway, red wings
    in a storefront tableau, lustrous, the live macaws

preening, beaks opening and closing
  like those animated knives that unfold all night
    in jewellers' windows. For sale,

glass eyes turned out toward the rain,
  the birds lined up like the endless flowers
    and cheap gems, the makeshift tables

of secondhand magazines
  and shoes the hawkers eye
    while they shelter in the doorways of banks.

So many pockets and paper cups
  and hands reeled over the weight
    of that glittered pavement, and at 103rd

a woman reached to me across the wet roof
  of a stranger's car and said, *I'm Carlotta,
  I'm hungry.* She was only asking for change,

so I don't know why I took her hand.
  The rooftops were glowing above us,
    enormous, crystalline, a second city

lit from within. That night
  a man on the downtown local stood up
    and said, *My name is Ezekiel,*

I am a poet, and my poem this evening is called
  fall. He stood up straight
    to recite, a child reminded of his posture

by the gravity of his text, his hands
  hidden in the pockets of his coat.
    Love is protected, he said,

the way leaves are packed in snow,
  the rubies of fall. God is protecting
    the jewel of love for us.

He didn't ask for anything, but I gave him
  the change left in my pocket,
    and the man beside me, impulsive, moved,

gave Ezekiel his watch.
  It wasn't an expensive watch,
    I don't even know if it worked,

but the poet started, then walked away
  as if so much good fortune
    must be hurried away from,

before anyone realises it's a mistake.
  Carlotta, her stocking cap glazed
    like feathers in the rain,

under the radiant towers, the floodlit ramparts,
  must have wondered at my impulse to touch her,
    which was like touching myself,

the way your own hand feels when you hold it
   because you want to feel contained.
      She said, *You get home safe now, you hear?*

In the same way Ezekiel turned back
   to the benevolent stranger.
      I will write a poem for you tomorrow,

he said. *The poem I will write will go like this:*
   Our ancestors are replenishing
      the jewel of love for us.

CHANTEUSE

Prendergast painted the Public Garden;
remembered, even at a little distance,
the city takes on his ravishing tones.

Jots of colour resolve: massed parasols
above a glimmering pond, the transit
of almost translucent swans. Brilliant bits

– jewels? slices of sugared fruit? – bloom
into a clutch of skirts on the bridge
above the summer boaters. His city's essence:

all the hues of chintzes or makeup
or Italian ices, all the sheen artifice
is capable of. Our city's lavish paintbox.

Name the colours: light turning to rose,
a suspended glow, late afternoons,
in the air above the avenues,

as if the houses themselves were remembering,
their brick-tinted memory a warm haze
above the taxis and the homebound cars.

Almost the colour of the glow, evenings,
at the end of April, when one lamppost
positioned exactly right, on Marlboro Street,

would shine through the unfurled petals
of a blossoming magnolia, marbling
a corner mailbox, an iron gate,

a tract of sidewalk – light stained by the skin
of flowers, the shadows of bloom. I loved
that city, the two of us traversing

that light. Name the colours: the frothing pink
evidence of tulips beheaded in the Garden,
patinated rainstreaked green

of Dover Station's backstreet pagoda
rusting over the moon windows
of the Premier Diner, the surplus clothing store

of Harry the Greek – the Geek, everyone called him –
his windows painted over with the prices
of socks and trousers. What was our city

but wonderful detail? A scaffolding's
wrought-iron tiara, the evening's violet smoulder
over the avenue's noise and happy taxis.

Lit windows – possible futures
with their parchment glow, intimate interiors –
and then the brilliant red snow

of firecracker wrappings, Chinese New Year's
scatter of bright applause. Hammered copper
carp rising in a tank; beancakes in the baker's

window glazed in sugar water. A tangle
of crated squid. Flares, sparks shaking
the avenue awake, the tumbling fiery bolts

of blazing silk. Name the colour, the one
you've been saving, memory's glimmering
spotlight and sequin: once, upstairs

in a nearly empty room over a crowded bar,
a beautiful black drag queen – perched
on the edge of the piano, under a blue spot,

her legs crossed in front of her
so that the straps of her sparkling ankle shoes
glimmered – sang only to us. The song

was Rodgers and Hart – *My romance*
doesn't have to have a moon in the sky –
and she was perfect. The piano's slow unfolding,

her smoke-burnished, entirely believable voice,
the sequins on her silver bolero
shimmering ice blue. Cavafy ends a poem

of regret and desire – he had no other theme
than memory's erotics, his ashen atmosphere –
by going out onto a balcony

to change my thoughts at least
by seeing something of this city I love,
a little movement in the streets,

in the shops. That was all it took
to console him, some token of Alexandria's
anarchic life. How did it go on without him,

the city he'd transformed into feeling?
Hadn't he made it entirely
into himself? *High windy blue,* I wrote,

in one of those old notebooks one never
really reads again, *burning over the balconies.*
Whose city was it, Prendergast's,

Cavafy's, ours, the rapt singer
who caught us in the glory
of her artifice? One Christmas,

when the day broke every record
for warmth, we pried open our long-shut windows
above Beacon Street and the wind pouring

into that high-ceilinged room
swept every flake of paper snow
from the tree. We were awash in

a studio-sized blizzard, snow
on your sleeves and hair, and anything
that divided us then was bridged

by the sudden graceful shock
of being inside the warmest storm.
That is how I would describe her voice,

her lyric that becomes, now, my city:
torch, invitation, accomplishment. *My romance
doesn't need a blue lagoon standing by* . . .

As she invented herself, memory revises
and restores her, and the moment
she sang. I think we were perfected,

when we became her audience,
and maybe from that moment on
it didn't matter so much exactly

what would become of us.
I would say she *was* memory,
and we were restored by

the radiance of her illusion,
her consummate attention to detail,
– *name the colours* – her song: my Alexandria,

my romance, my magnolia
distilling lamplight, my backlit glory
of the wigshops, my haze

and glow, my torch, my skyrocket,
my city, my false,
my splendid chanteuse.

FOG

The crested iris by the front gate waves
its blue flags three days, exactly,

then they vanish. The peony buds'
tight wrappings are edged crimson;

when they open, a little blood-colour
will ruffle at the heart of the flounced,

unbelievable white. Three weeks after the test,
the vial filled from the crook

of my elbow, I'm seeing blood everywhere:
a casual nick from the garden shears,

a shaving cut and I feel the physical rush
of the welling up, the wine-fountain

dark as Siberian iris. The thin green porcelain
teacup, our homemade Ouija's planchette,

rocks and wobbles every night, spins
and spells. It seems a cloud of spirits

numerous as lilac panicles vie for occupancy –
children grabbing for the telephone,

happy to talk to someone who isn't dead yet?
Everyone wants to speak at once, or at least

these random words appear, incongruous
and exactly spelled: *energy, immunity, kiss.*

Then: *M. has immunity. W. has.*
And that was all. One character, Frank,

distinguishes himself: a boy who lived
in our house in the thirties, loved dogs

and gangster movies, longs for a body,
says he can watch us through the television,

asks us to stand before the screen
and kiss. *God in garden*, he says.

Sitting out on the back porch at twilight,
I'm almost convinced. In this geometry

of paths and raised beds, the green shadows
of delphinium, there's an unseen rustling:

some secret amplitude
seems to open in this orderly space.

Maybe because it contains so much dying,
all these tulip petals thinning

at the base until any wind takes them.
I doubt anyone else would see that, looking in,

and then I realise my garden has no outside, only *is*
subjectively. As blood is utterly without

an outside, can't be seen except out of context,
the wrong colour in alien air, no longer itself.

Though it submits to test, two,
to be exact, each done three times,

though not for me, since at their first entry
into my disembodied blood

there was nothing at home there.
For you they entered the blood garden over

and over, like knocking at a door
because you know someone's home. Three times

the Elisa Test, three the Western Blot,
and then the incoherent message. We're

the public health care worker's
nine o'clock appointment,

she is a phantom hand who forms
the letters of your name, and the word

that begins with *P.* I'd lie out
and wait for the god if it weren't

so cold, the blue moon huge
and disruptive above the flowering crab's

foaming collapse. The spirits say *Fog*
when they can't speak clearly

and the letters collide; sometimes
for them there's nothing outside the mist

of their dying. Planchette,
peony, I would think of anything

not to say the word. Maybe the blood
in the flower is a god's. Kiss me,

in front of the screen, please,
the dead are watching.

They haven't had enough yet.
Every new bloom is falling apart.

I would say anything else
in the world, any other word.

THE WARE COLLECTION OF GLASS FLOWERS AND FRUIT, HARVARD MUSEUM

Strange paradise, complete with worms,
monument of an obsessive will to fix forms;
every apricot or yellow spot's seen so closely,
in these blown blooms and fruit, that exactitude

is not quite imitation. Leaf and root,
the sweet flag's flaring bud already,
at the tip, blackened: it's hard to remember
these were ballooned and shaped by breath.

They're lovely because they *seem*
to decay: blue spots on bluer plums,
mould tarring a striped rose. I don't want to admire
the glassblower's academic replica,

his copies correct only to a single sense.
And why did a god so invested in permanence
choose so fragile a medium, the last material
he might expect to last? Better prose

to tell the forms of things, or illustration.
Though there's something seductive in this
    impossibility:
transparent colour telling the live mottle of peach,
the blush or tint of crab, englobed,

gorgeous, edible. How else match that flush?
He's built a perfection out of hunger,
fused layer upon layer, swirled until
what can't be tasted, won't yield,

almost satisfies, an art
mouthed to the shape of how soft things are,
how good, before they disappear.

THE WINGS

The bored child at the auction
lies in his black rainboots reading,
on the grass, while beneath the tent

his parents grow rich with witness:
things that were owned once, in place,
now must be cared for, carried

to the block. A coast of cloud
becomes enormous, above the wet field,
while the auctioneer holds up

now the glass lily severed
from its epergne, now the mother-of-pearl
lorgnette. These things require

the boy's parents so much they don't know
where he is, which is gone: the book
he's brought, swords on its slick cover,

promises more than objects or storm.
He's lost in the story a while
but then the sun comes out,

he's been reading a long time,
and he lies on his side with his cheek
against the grass. This seems

the original moment of restless dreaming:
shiny rubber boots, a book forgotten
in one hand, a tired reader's face pressed

against damp green. He's the newest thing here.
I've bought a dark-varnished painting
of irises, a dead painter's bouquet

penciled, precisely, *Laura M.*
1890. The woman in front of us has bid
for a dead woman's plates, iridescent flocks

of blue birds under glaze. When it's all over
his parents awaken the sleeping reader:
his father's bought a pair of snowshoes

nearly as tall as the boy, who slings them both
over his back and thus is suddenly winged.
His face fills with purpose;

the legendary heroes put away in his satchel,
he's become useful again, he's moved
back into the world of things

to be accomplished: an angel
to carry home the narrative of our storied,
scattering things.

★

Didn't you want apples on the branch,
not just the cold-scented globes
but winesap or some sharp red
ballooning from the bearing wood?

And didn't we find, on Saturday morning,
at the edge of town,
beside a barn twisting
on its foundations, trying to collapse,

an abandoned orchard
offering branch after branch,
the ones a little higher
than the deer could reach?

Everywhere under the trees
long flattened grasses
where they'd lain, gorged with the low
or windfall fruit. We cut an armload,

trying to jostle nothing loose,
swearing at the sweet ringing
when any one fell –
strange how a solid thing

chimes. In a barn down the road
– among the oily lawnmowers,
the cracked motors, sapbuckets
and gaskets – a rabbit cage,

two rough-cut painted pine hares
bracing a pen of chicken wire,
their red eyes eager and intent:
a beautiful thing, made for the loved companion

of a loved child, ours for two dollars
and irreplaceable. We brought it home,
with the few intact apple branches
and a sheaf of maple burning

the unmatchable colour things come to
when the green goes out of them
and the rippling just under
blooms through. Some days things yield

such grace and complexity that what we see
seems offered. I can't stop thinking
about the German film in which the angels
– who exist outside of time and thus long

for things that take place –
love most of all human stories,
the way we tell ourselves
what we dread or wish.

Of all our locations
their favourite is the library;
the director pictures them perched
on the balustrades, clustering

on the stairs, bent over
the solitary readers as if
to urge us on, to say *Here,*
have you looked here yet?

★

If endlessness offered itself to me today
I don't think I'd have done anything

differently. I was looking from the car window
at the unlikely needlepoint wild asters made

of an October slope, blue starry heads
heaped upon each other, too wet and heavy

with their own completion to stand.
I didn't even stop, but that brief

yellow-eyed punctuation in a field
gone violet and golden at once,

sudden and gone, is more than I can say.
There's simply no way to get it right,

and it was just one thing. Holsteins,
a little down the road, paraded

toward the evening's expected comforts;
two cats in the long grass

observed. By a rowboat-sized pond,
one slanting ram floated on the thinnest legs.

There were geese. *There were:*
the day's narration is simple assertion;

it's enough to name the instances.
Don't let anybody tell you

death's the price exacted
for the ability to love;

couldn't we live forever
without running out of occasions?

★

In the Exhibition Hall each unfurled
three-by-five field bears
in awkward or accomplished embroidery

a name, every banner stitched to another
and another. They're reading
the unthinkable catalogue of the names,

so many they blur, become
a single music pronounced with difficulty
over the microphone, become a pronoun,

become You. It's the clothing I can't get past,
the way a favourite pair of jeans,
a striped shirt's sewn onto the cloth;

the fading, the pulls in the fabric
demonstrate how these relics formed around
one essential, missing body.

An empty pair of pants
is mortality's severest evidence.
Embroidered mottoes blend

into something elegaic but removed;
a shirt can't be remote.
One can't look past

the sleeves where two arms
were, where a shoulder pushed
against a seam, and someone knew exactly

how the stitches pressed against skin
that can't be generalised but was,
irretrievably, you, or yours.

★

In September the garden
– this ordered enactment of desire –
is exhilarating again;

the new season says
Look what can be done, says
any mistake can be rectified:

the too-shaded lavender
transplanted to a brighter bed,
a lilac standard bought

and planted in a spot
requiring height, strong form.
Setting them in place,

attending to the settling of roots
between yellowed iris
and flourishing asters,

I'm making an angel,
like those Arcimboldos where the human profile
is all berry and leaf,

the specific character of bloom
assembled into an overriding form.
And then the bulbs: the slim-necked tulips

such saints of patience, exploding
so long after you plant them
they're nearly forgotten. Ignore

or attend, the same thing happens:
buried wishes become blooms,
supple and sheened as skin. I'm thinking

of the lily-flowered kind
on slim spines, the ones
that might as well be flames,

just two slight wings that will
blaze into the future;
I have to think they have a will,

a design so inherent in the cells
nothing could subtract from them
the least quotient of grace,

or wish to. I dreamed,
the night after the fall planting,
that a bird who loved me

had been long neglected, and when
I took it from the closet and gave it water
its tongue began to move again,

and it began to beat the lush green music
of its wings, and wrapped the brilliant risk
of leaves all around my face.

★

We've been out again on the backroads,
buying things. Here's a permanent harvest:
an apple and four cherries
stencilled on a chair-back,

the arm-wood glowing, so human,
from within, where the red paint's
been worn away by how many arms
at rest. Polished and placed

by the blue table and the windows
that frame the back garden,
it's a true consolation,
necessary, become *this*

through its own wearing away
by use, festive with its once-bright
fruit. Anything lived into long enough
becomes an orchard.

And I've bought a book printed
in Edinburgh, in 1798 – where's it been,

clearly never much referred to,
two hundred years? Bound in whorled leather,

it's the second volume of a concordance
of biblical nouns, *A Literal,*
Critical and Systematic Description of Objects
in fine and oddly comforting raised type:

SADNESS, by means of which the heart
is made better, weaned
from worldly things. And *THE LIMIT*
of God's house, round about, being most holy

imports that even the most circumstantial things
are holy in themselves: contradictory,
and heretical, for this eighteenth-century John Brown,
whom the foxed title page identifies only as

'Minister of the Gospels at Haddington.'
In my afternoon class the students
sit in a circle of chairs on the terrace,
and behind their faces, which seem then

so dizzingly new, all the rich
commingling of leaves hurry downward
into latent shades too subtle
to ever name, colours

we perhaps can't register even once,
and they wonder why the poet we're reading's
so insistent on mortality. I want to tell them
how I make the angel, that form

between us and the unthinkable,
that face we give the empty ringing,

and how that form for me appears in a boy
with snowshoe wings slung across his shoulders,

or in the child sprawled on the marble floor
of the post office yesterday,
who filled the echoing lobby with random notes
blown on her recorder, music made out of waiting.

I let the light-glazed angel
in the children's bodies, the angel
with his face flushed in the heat
of recognising any birth,

I let him bend over my desk and speak
in a voice so assured you wouldn't know
that anyone was dying. *Any music's
made of waiting*, he says.

I make him again. *Look,
it doesn't matter so much.
See into what you can.*
I make the angel lean over our bed

in the next room, where you're sleeping
the sturdy, uncompromised sleep
of someone going to work early tomorrow.
I am willing around you, hard,

the encompassing wings of the one called
unharmed. His name is nowhere
in the concordance, but I don't care;
he's the rationale for any naming.

A steady fine-pointed rain's
etching the new plantings,

and I'm making the rain
part of the angel. *Try to be certain,*

he says, where you're looking.
If you're offered endlessness,
don't do anything differently. The rule
of earth is attachment:

here what can't be held
is. You die by dying
into what matters, which will kill you,
but first it'll be enough. Or more than that:

your story, which you have worn away
as you shaped it,
which has become itself
as it has disappeared.

DIFFERENCE

The jellyfish   *THE RIPE? SLACK COUNTRY LASS*
float in the bay shallows *SLIPS THROUGH MY ARMS*
like schools of clouds,   *LIKE A SHEAF OF ___ WHEAT.*

                                D.H. LAWRENCE

a dozen identical – is it right
to call them creatures,
these elaborate sacks

of nothing? All they seem
is shape, and shifting,
and though a whole troop

of undulant cousins
go about their business
within a single wave's span,

every one does something unlike:
this one a balloon
open on both ends

but swollen to its full expanse,
this one a breathing heart,
this a pulsing flower.

This one a rolled condom,
or a plastic purse swallowing itself,
that one a Tiffany shade,

this a troubled parasol.
This submarine opera's
all subterfuge and disguise,

its plot a fabulous tangle
of hiding and recognition:
nothing but trope,

nothing but something
forming itself into figures
then refiguring,

sheer ectoplasm
recognisable only as the stuff
of metaphor. What can words do

but link what we know
to what we don't,
and so form a shape?

Which shrinks or swells,
configures or collapses, blooms
even as it is described

into some unlikely
marine chiffon:
a gown for Isadora?

Nothing but style.
What binds
one shape to another

also sets them apart
– but what's lovelier
than the shapeshifting

transparence of *like* and *as:*
clear, undulant words?
We look at alien grace,

unfettered
by any fixed form,
and we say: balloon, flower,

heart, condom, opera,
lampshade, parasol, ballet.
Hear how the mouth,

so full
of longing for the world,
changes its shape?

THE ADVENT CALENDARS

These were our first instruction
  in the power of the unopened.
They're lined up tonight
  edge to edge, a city of tiny windows

behind this small town shop's
  breath-steamed glass: frosty barns,
Bavarian villages, diluted Breughels
  where children sled on the slope

above the bridge, an owl nests
  in the high window of an attic.
Lamps in every kitchen.
  First you must find *One*,

the hidden world's premiere,
  a door which always gives onto
something minor. Then come days
  of incidental scenes, patient animals,

the entr'acte of miracle.
  Eventually – *Twelve*, say –
there's perhaps a shepherd boy
  washing down the stable floor,

a milkmaid bent over the earth's
  whitest treasure. Number after number
prolongs anticipation: *Sixteen*,
  an out-of-season dove carrying

a wisp of straw, quarried
  from what bank of snow; *Twenty-one*,
a kitten who's upset a saucer
  set out on the chilly flagstones.

About the final miracle,
   there's little surprise,
once you've seen it; you don't need
   to believe the story about space

pouring itself into the form
   of a god, the glory in the barn.
It's the promise that matters,
   the twenty-five portals

incomplete until they're opened
   but then incomplete still,
since their charm lay in concealment.
   Moments from now we'll walk

our street's corridor of lit
   and darkened houses,
the exhaust-dimmed façades
   brightened by storm, interiors revealed

a window at a time, if at all.
   Nights like this
our town grows smaller,
   compressed under the freighted weather,

suspended white cargo sifting
   equally all night onto roofs
and lilacs, fenceposts and streets.
   We're the shook heart of the paperweight,

the glass village falling forever
   through the steady arms
of the snow, which touch us,
   each pair, just once,

then let us go. Each particular's
   erased, exact form abstracted
into shape, the world gone
   general, unmoored, white.

Is God also in the absence
   of detail? The unlit spaces
between houses are thick with snow,
   but here and there a window's glow

illumines a steady shaft of falling,
   one perfect rhythm of hesitation:
the snow is an old, old story,
   in no hurry to be told.

Half the windows are open,
   half the windows closed.
There is no single location of miracle.

TO BESSIE DRENNAN

Because she could find no one else to paint a picture of the old family place where she and her sisters lived . . . she attended an adult education class in Montpelier. In one evening Bessie Drennan learned everything she would need to accomplish her goals . . .

The Vermont Folklife Center Newsletter

Bessie, you've made space dizzy
with your perfected technique for snow:
white spatters and a dry brush
feathering everything in the world

seem to make the firmament fly.
Four roads converge on the heart of town,
this knot of white and yellow houses
angling off kilter, their astigmatic windows

almost all in rows. Lucky the skater
threading the yellow tavern's quilt-sized pond,
the yellow dogs who punctuate the village
where our occupations are chasing

and being chaste, sleighing and sledding
and snowshoeing from house to house
in our conical, flamelike hats.
Even the barns are sliding in snow,

though the birches are all golden
and one maple blazes without being consumed.
Is it from a hill nearby we're watching,
or somewhere in the sky? Could we be flying

on slick runners down into the village?
Is that mare with the elegant legs
truly the size of a house,
and is this the store where everyone bought

those pointed hats, the snowshoes that angle
in contradictory directions?
Isn't that Rin Tin Tin, bigtongued
and bounding and in two places at once?

Down there in the world's corner two children
steal away onto the frozen pond,
carrying their toboggan. Even the weathervanes
– bounding fish, a sailing stag – look happy.

The houses are swaying, Bessie,
and nothing is grounded in shadow,
set loose by weather and art
from gravity's constraints.

And though I think this man is falling,
is it anything but joyous,
the arc his red scarf
transcribes in the air?

NO

The children have brought their wood turtle
into the dining hall
because they want us to feel

the power they have
when they hold a house
in their own hands, want us to feel

alien lacquer and the little thrill
that he might, like God, show his face.
He's the colour of ruined wallpaper,

of cognac, and he's closed,
pulled in as though he'll never come out;
nothing shows but the plummy leather

of the legs, his claws resembling clusters
of diminutive raspberries.
They know he makes night

anytime he wants, so perhaps
he feels at the centre of everything,
as they do. His age,

greater than that of anyone
around the table, is a room
from which they are excluded,

though they don't mind,
since they can carry this perfect
building anywhere. They love

that he might poke out
his old, old face, but doesn't.
I think the children smell unopened,

like unlit candles, as they heft him
around the table, praise his secrecy,
holding to each adult face

his prayer,
the single word of the shell,
which is no.

BRILLIANCE

Maggie's taking care of a man
who's dying; he's attended to everything,
said goodbye to his parents,

paid off his credit card.
She says *Why don't you just
run it up to the limit?*

but he wants everything
squared away, no balance owed,
though he misses the pets

he's already found a home for
– he can't be around dogs or cats,
too much risk. He says,

I can't have anything.
She says, *A bowl of goldfish?*
He says he doesn't want to start

with anything and then describes
the kind he'd maybe like,
how their tails would fan

to a gold flaring. They talk
about hot jewel tones,
gold lacquer, say maybe

they'll go pick some out
though he can't go much of anywhere and then
abruptly he says *I can't love*

anything I can't finish.
He says it like he's had enough
of the whole scintillant world,

though what he means is
he'll never be satisfied and therefore
has established this discipline,

a kind of severe rehearsal.
That's where they leave it,
him looking out the window,

her knitting as she does because
she needs to do something.
Later he leaves a message:

Yes to the bowl of goldfish.
Meaning: let me go, if I have to,
in brilliance. In a story I read,

a Zen master who'd perfected
his detachment from the things of the world
remembered, at the moment of dying,

a deer he used to feed in the park,
and wondered who might care for it,
and at that instant was reborn

in the stunned flesh of a fawn.
So, Maggie's friend –
is he going out

into the last loved object
of his attention?
Fanning the veined translucence

of an opulent tail,
undulant in some uncapturable curve,
is he bronze chrysanthemums,

copper leaf, hurried darting,
doubloons, icon-coloured fins
troubling the water?

BILL'S STORY

When my sister came back from Africa,
we didn't know at first how everything
had changed. After a while Annie
bought men's and boys' clothes in all sizes,
and filled her closets with little
or huge things she could never wear.

Then she took to buying out
theatrical shops, rental places on the skids,
sweeping in and saying, *I'll take everything.*
Dementia was the first sign of something
we didn't even have a name for,
in 1978. She was just becoming stranger

- all those clothes, the way she'd dress me up
when I came to visit. It was like we could go back
to playing together again, and get it right.
She was a performance artist, and she did
her best work then, taking the clothes to clubs,
talking, putting them all on, talking.

It was years before she was in the hospital,
and my mother needed something
to hold onto, some way to be helpful,
so she read a book called *Deathing*
(a cheap, ugly verb if ever I heard one)
and took its advice to heart;

she'd sit by the bed and say, *Annie,
look for the light, look for the light.*
It was plain that Anne did not wish
to be distracted by these instructions;
she came to, though she was nearly gone then,

and looked at our mother with what was almost
  certainly

annoyance. *It's a white light,*
Mom said, and this struck me
as incredibly presumptuous, as if the light
we'd all go into would be just the same.
Maybe she wanted to give herself up
to indigo, or red. If we can barely even speak

to each other, living so separately,
how can we all die the same?
I used to take the train to the hospital,
and sometimes the only empty seats
would be the ones that face backwards.
I'd sit there and watch where I'd been

waver and blur out, and finally
I liked it, seeing what you've left
get more beautiful, less specific.
Maybe her light was all that gaberdine
and flannel, khaki and navy
and silk and stripes. If you take everything,

you've got to let everything go. Dying
must take more attention than I ever imagined.
Just when she'd compose herself
and seem fixed on the work before her,
Mother would fret, trying to help her
just one more time: *Look for the light,*

until I took her arm
and told her wherever I was in the world
I would come back, no matter how difficult
it was to reach her, if I heard her calling.
Shut up, mother, I said, and Annie died.

NIGHT FERRY

We're launched into the darkness,
half a load of late passengers
   gliding onto the indefinite
     black surface, a few lights vague

and shimmering on the island shore.
Behind us, between the landing's twin flanks
   (wooden pylons strapped with old tyres),
     the docklights shatter in our twin,

folding wakes, their colours
on the roughened surface combed
   like the patterns of Italian bookpaper,
     lustrous and promising. The narrative

of the ferry begins and ends brilliantly,
and its text is this moving out
   into what is soon before us
     and behind: the night going forward,

sentence by sentence, as if on faith,
into whatever takes place.
   It's strange how we say things *take place*,
     as if occurrence were a location –

the dark between two shores,
for instance, where for a little while
   we're on no solid ground. Twelve minutes,
     precisely, the night ferry hurries

across the lake. And what happens
is always the body of water,

its skin like the wrong side of satin.
    I love to stand like this,

    where the prow pushes blunt into the future,
knowing, more than seeing, how
    the surface rushes and doesn't even break
        but simply slides under us.

    Lake melds into shoreline,
one continuous black moiré;
    the boatmen follow the one course they know
        toward a dock nearly the mirror

    of the first, mercury lamps vapouring
over the few late birds
    attending the pier. Even the bored men
        at the landing, who wave

    their flashlights for the last travellers,
steering us toward the road, will seem
    the engineers of our welcome,
        their red-sheathed lights marking

    the completion of our, or anyone's, crossing.
Twelve dark minutes. Love,
    we are between worlds, between
        unfathomed water and I don't know how much

    light-flecked black sky, the fogged circles
of island lamps. I am almost not afraid
    on this good boat, breathing its good smell
        of grease and kerosene,

    warm wind rising up the stairwell
from the engine's serious study.

There's no beautiful binding
  for this story, only the temporary,

  liquid endpapers of the hurried water,
shot with random colour. But in the gliding forward's
  a scent so quick and startling
    it might as well be blowing

  off the stars. Now, just before we arrive,
the wind carries a signal and a comfort,
  lovely, though not really meant for us:
    woodsmoke risen from the chilly shore.

BECOMING A MEADOW

A bookstore in a seaside town,
the beginning of February, off season,
and snow outside the book-filled glass hurries down

and turns in whorls above the frozen
street, blurring the boarded storefronts (taffy, souvenirs),
tattooing the water with the storm's million

fingerprints. Gusts billow over the empty pier.
Someone comes in and the bell on the shop door rings;
then the words I hear in my head, from nowhere,

are *becoming a meadow.* Why does that jangling
shopkeeper's music translate itself to that phrase?
Yesterday morning we walked a beach where the tide
  angled

and broke in beautiful loops, the waves'
endless rows of bold cursive
one atop the other, scrawling an exercise page

of *O*s in a copybook the world's never tired of.
A place called Head of the Meadow.
I don't know how to say how perfect it was,

though it was only a short walk; the morning was cold,
we hadn't brought enough to wear.
For weeks I've been turning over and over

one barely articulated question; here,
among the cultivated disorder of the book-rows,
the words present themselves as a sort of answer:

a meadow accepts itself as various, allows
some parts of itself to always be going away,
because whatever happens in that blown,

ragged field of grass and sway
is the meadow, and threading the frost
of its unlikely brilliance yesterday

we also were the meadow. In the bookstore
while you are reading and I am allowing myself
simply to be comforted by the presence of stories,

the bound, steady presences on the shelves,
fixed as nothing else is, I am thinking of my terror
of decay, the little hell opening in every violated cell,

the virus tearing
away — is it? — and we are still a part of the meadow
because I am thinking of it, hearing

the bell-phrase of it: Head of the Meadow
in my head. The titles of the books,
the letters of the writers' names blow

like grasses, become individual stalks,
seedheads, burrs, rimed swell
of dune on which the beachgrass is writing its book

in characters unreadable or read:
the meadow-book
you are writing, and which you read.

And then the whole place, the narrow aisles and stacks,
is one undulant, salt-swollen meadow of water,
one filling and emptying wave, spilling and pulling back,

and everything waves are: dissolving, faster,
only to swell again, like the baskets of bread
and fish in the story, the miracle baskets.

And if one wave breaking says
You're dying, then the rhythm and shift of the whole
says nothing about endings, and half the shawling head

of each wave's spume pours into the trough
of the one before,
and half blows away in spray, backward, toward the open
    sea.

WITH ANIMALS

Wet grass, headlights streaking morning fog,
    and three deer sudden in my friends' driveway:

lithe buck leaping in seconds
    onto the stone embankment, flash of doe following,

then the slimhipped adolescent, mossy antlers
    sprouting . . . So much hurrying life in them,

glancing off the human world,
    like the herons I used to watch in the country,

the morning's steel-feathered news
    poised on the single lip of rock

cresting the river, upright, each a yard
    of oystery shantung, fog-toned, lyrical

and awkward at once. In air they were fire,
    that easy, over the railroad shacks where dawn

broke the pearl veil of acres and acres
    of fog. Then they were gone for days, and gone

all winter. From those steep-raked hills
    so many bells rang, and nights when it snowed

it was as if the tolling were hung
    in the air over town, the chiming

actually vibrating through each snowflake
    until the bells would reverberate

against the granite hillside
  and the frozen surface of the river

whose banks had grown together, all November,
  as ice moved up from the cataract,

through which the bells rang also,
  ice doubling them again.

The colder the night the more perfectly the air
  itself seemed to ring, the whole storm

swirling around us. My dog would stand
  caught in that sound, absolutely still,

while the ringing passed through his solid
  year-old body and he would look up,

head cocked slightly, as if for an explanation.
  That winter, just to feel I owned something,

I drove once a week to our cabin in the woods.
  Something chimed from the thickets one January
   morning

like a bird continuing the hammer of its call
  over and over without stirring from its branch,

and I followed the sound until I could see
  from the road – I don't want to tell this –

what looked like a nest, a cluster of necks
  moving back and forth above the snow.

And I crouched into the brush
and saw what called: four paws thrust up

from a hole the heat of a body had melted;
it must have been lying there all night,

running on its back. The hole was wider,
close to the soil, and the animal's face

was hidden by snow. I thought, *It's a fox,
don't touch it*, I thought *touch it*. At first

I covered its face, as if that would help it die,
but I couldn't do it, I scraped the snow away,

all of it, from its face: someone's
fox-coloured housedog, a dustcloth of a dog.

And feeling half foolish and half entirely real
I said *You can go if you want to,*

it's all right if you want to go.
The dog never even looked at me, the dog

kept running almost mechanically, on its back
in the stained nest, all four paws moving

in that pointless version of flight, nodding
its head from side to side and making the little

choked sound, at exactly the same interval.
That was what it could do. I didn't know

it had been shot in the head, as country people
will do, when an animal has outlived its usefulness;

the man or boy with the rifle hadn't cared
to make sure it was dead. It wasn't dead.

It wanted even a life reduced to this
twitching repetition, no matter how diminished,

how brutal, how wrong. Something which was
and was not the dog wanted to continue,

something entirely dependent upon that body
which was already beginning to be rimed

with ice. Something cleaves to form
until the last minute, past it,

and though the vet's needle was an act
of mercy, the life needed to continue,

the life was larger than cruelty,
the life denied the obliterating gesture

where only kindness had been expected.
Even with one eye shot away and the brain spasming

the life takes it in and says *more*,
just as it takes in the quick jab of the needle

and the flooding darkness. The life doesn't care.
The life only wants, the fugitive life.

LAMENT-HEAVEN

What hazed around the branches
    late in March was white at first,
        as if a young tree's ghost

were blazing in the woods,
    a fluttering around the limbs
        like shredded sleeves. A week later,

green fountaining,
    frothing champagne;
        against the dark of evergreen,

that skyrocket shimmer. I think
    this is how our deaths would look,
        seen from a great distance,

if we could stand that far
    from ourselves: the way birch leaves
        signal and flash, candling

into green then winking out.
    You've seen lights along the shore
        move forward and recede,

not knowing if any single one were house
    or buoy, lamp or reflection:
        all one fabric. If death's like that,

if we are continuous,
    rippling from nothing into being,
        then why can't we let ourselves go

into the world's shimmering story?
   Who can become lost in a narrative,
      if all he can think of is the end?

Only lights in a lapping harbour –
   nothing to fear – rising again,
      going out. No,

faster than that

★

like the carnival we saw one night,
   late, off the freeway on the South Shore,
      countless circuits of lightbulbs

hazing through thickening spring fog,
   the ferris wheel's phosphorescent roulette
      fog-haloed, blazing.

Then letters blinking on –
   G – H – O – S – T –
      and the linked cursive of *train:*

a funhouse locomotive of spirits,
   passengers on the white air?
      Our guiding spirit,

spelling out his name and intention
   through the Ouija's rainbowed alphabet,
      isn't much help. Though death's

his single subject,
   he insists there is none,
      or rather that what awaits us is 'home',

something he'll say little about.
  What does he mean –
    the cloudy parlours of heaven

or the insubstantial stuff of earth:
  an amusement park alien in its glitter,
    the mud-fragrant woods, soaked.

tonight, in spring rain,
  warm and unlikely?
    He won't answer.

He says death is peace.
  I don't believe a word he spells;
    I don't believe the lamenting

stops at the borders of this world
  or any other. Why give a ghost letters
    and the twin poles of yes and no;

isn't everything so shadowed
  by its own brevity
    we can barely tell the thing

from its elegy? Strip something
  of its mortality, and how do you know
    what's left to see?

★

In SingSing, on a chapel bulletin board,
  I read a sign someone spent hours lettering,
    the careful tattoo-on-paper

of a man with all the time
  in the world to make his point,
    text ringed around a Maltese cross:

72

God's not dead. I can 'feel' him
    all over me. In those miles of corridors
        men move from lock

to lock like canal water,
    each segment of hallway filling
        until the sluice gates open

and they pour into the next hall,
    so much black and blue water
        hurrying toward the shabby visitors' trailer.

My friend there says
    it's hard for him to write
        because so many men narrate

day and night the endless
    distracting monologues that keep them
        real: *I am here,*

doing this. I don't know
    how you could feel anything
        on your skin in there –

blows maybe, but not divinity.
    It's quiet here, I'm free to walk
        anywhere I want and nothing's touching me

that I'm certain I'd call endless,
    though I'd like to tell whoever inked
        that sign the truth, how last week

I felt this – godliness? –
    around me, in the enormous church

in Copley Square, under the gold-ribbed
vault

pierced by figured windows.
   A girl, twelve maybe, was playing the violin,
      rapturously, though I suppose for her

it was not trance but discipline
   that made the music gather and then tumble
      like water collecting in a fountain,

all hesitation and sudden release.
   The organist who accompanied
      would stop her, from time to time,

and together they'd repeat a phrase,
   and then the music would seem to fall forward,
      tumbling snowmelt breaking loose

from the hidden place
   where it had been contained.
      She was a black girl,

with large round glasses which she pushed
   closer to her eyes each time she paused.
      I would have lived in that music,

or rather it was as if I had been once
   the cautious and splendid cascade from the
   violin.
      It was the sound that movement

through experience would make,
   if we could stand far enough away
      to hear it: lovely, and unconsoling,

74

each phrase played out
    into a dense thicket of variations,
        into its web of meanings, lifted

and reconsidered, articulated
    into exhaustion, hurried and then stilled,
        a crowd of wings. I can't remember

even the melody, which doesn't matter;
    there's nothing to hold
        but the memory of the sensation

of such moments, cancelling out
    the whine of the self
        that doesn't want to be ground down,

answering the little human cry
    at the heart of the elegy,
        Oh why aren't I what I wanted to be,

exempt from history?
    The music mounts up,
        assembles its architecture

larger than any of us
    and doesn't need you to continue.
        Do you understand me?

I heard it, the music
    that could not go on without us,
        and I was inconsolable.

NOTES

'Demolition' is for David Wojahn. The poem is set, in part, at the home of August Saint-Gaudens in Cornish, New Hampshire, where models of the sculptor's works are displayed, including the maquette for the monument to Colonel Shaw in the Boston Common.

'Almost Blue' is for Lynda Hull.

'Broadway' is for Jean Valentine.

The quotation from Cavafy in 'Chanteuse' is from Edmund Keeley and Philip Sherard's translation of the *Collected Poems*.

'Brilliance' is for Maggie Valentine.

'Lament-Heaven' is titled after a phrase in Stephen Mitchell's translation of Rilke's 'Orpheus. Eurydice. Hermes', in which Rilke writes that the lament of Orpheus for Eurydice is such that from it arises a world of lamentation, and above that a 'lament-heaven, with its own disfigured stars.'